Praise t

"I am thankful for Jeremy and his desire for the church to experience the gift of community. This is a great resource to put in your leaders' hands to make the promise of life-giving community more attainable."

> **Brad House**, Executive Pastor, Sojourn Community
> Church, Louisville, KY, and author of *Community:*
> *Taking Your Small Groups Off Life Support*

"*Life-Giving Groups* is a biblically-based field manual for developing spiritually healthy multiplying small groups in your church. This tool has been written and refined over a ten-year period of personal experience and practice. Jeremy offers not only a proven model but also his rich insights and thoughtful perspectives for cultivating authentic community and discipleship."

> **Bill Wellons**, Founding Pastor, Fellowship Bible
> Church, Little Rock, AR

"Jeremy Linneman is a seasoned practitioner and coach in groups ministry. This book is a surgical tool that will help ministry leaders move their community from good intentions to wise implementation. I'm very excited to see this resource go viral for the future of mature and multiplying missionary communities."

> **Brandon Shields**, Lead Pastor, Soma Church,
> Indianapolis, IN

"Jeremy's heart for making and multiplying disciples comes through loud and clear in *Life-Giving Groups*. I share his conviction that groups are the best place for people to grow in Christ-likeness. Whether your church is just starting a small group ministry or looking to breathe fresh life into your existing ministry, this book is a practical, accessible guide to deeper, richer community."

> **Scott Hickox**, Lead Pastor, The Journey Church West County, St. Louis, MO

"During Jeremy's time as our Pastor of Community Life, our community groups not only doubled in size, but they grew in depth, health, and sustainability. This is a great, practical resource for anyone who is trying to build a healthy, multiplying group culture."

> **Kevin Jamison**, Lead Pastor, Sojourn Community Church East, Louisville, KY

"Jeremy is a thought leader in the context of the local church and community groups. Anybody who is interested in developing healthy, multiplying, gospel-centered group life will benefit from this new book."

> **JT English**, Pastor of The Village Institute, The Village Church, Flower Mound, TX

Praise for the "How-To" Series

"The Sojourn Network 'How-To' books are a great combination of biblical theology and practical advice, driven by a commitment to the gospel and the local congregation. Written by the local church for the local church — just the job!"

> **Tim Chester**, pastor of Grace Church Boroughbridge, faculty member of Crosslands Training, and author of over 40 books

"This series brings pastoral wisdom for everyday life in the church of Jesus Christ. Think of these short, practical books as the equivalent of a healthy breakfast, a sandwich and apple for lunch, and a family enjoying dinner together. The foundational theology is nutritious, and the practical applications will keep the body strong."

> **Dr. David Powlison**, Executive Director of CCEF; senior editor, Journal of Biblical Counseling; author of *Good and Angry: Redeeming Anger* and *Making All Things New: Restoring Joy to the Sexually Broken*

"Most leaders don't need another abstract book on leadership; we need help with the 'how-to's.' And my friends in the Sojourn Network excel in this area. I've been well served by their practical ministry wisdom, and I know you will be too."

> **Bob Thune**, Founding Pastor, Coram Deo Church, Omaha, NE, author of *Gospel Eldership* and co-author of *The Gospel-Centered Life*

"I cannot express strong enough what a valuable resource this is for church planters, church planting teams and young churches. The topics that are addressed in these books are so needed in young churches. I have been in ministry and missions for over 30 years and I learned a lot from reading. Very engaging and very practical!"

Larry McCrary, Co-Founder and Director of The Upstream Collective

"There are many aspects of pastoral ministry that aren't (and simply can't) be taught in seminary. Even further, many pastors simply don't have the benefit of a brotherhood of pastors that they can lean on to help them navigate topics such as building a healthy plurality of elders or working with artists in the church. I'm thankful for the men and women who labored to produce this series, which is both theologically-driven and practically-minded. The Sojourn Network "How-To" series is a great resource for pastors and church planters alike."

Jamaal Williams, Lead Pastor of Sojourn Midtown, Louisville, KY

"HOW-TO" GROW HEALTHY,
MULTIPLYING COMMUNITY GROUPS

LIFE-Giving GROUPS

Jeremy Linneman

Series Editor: Dave Harvey

Life-Giving Groups
"How-To" Grow Healthy, Multiplying Community Groups

© 2018 Jeremy Linneman
All rights reserved.

A publication of Sojourn Network Press in Louisville, KY. For more books by Sojourn Network, visit us at sojournnetwork.com/store.

Cover design: Josh Noom & Benjamin Vrbicek
Interior design: Benjamin Vrbicek

Trade paperback ISBN: 978-1732055216

The Sojourn Network book series is dedicated to the pastors, elders, and deacons of Sojourn Network churches. Because you are faithful, the church will be served and sent as we plant, grow, and multiply healthy churches that last.

CONTENTS

Series Preface vii

Introductory Letter 1

1. Philosophy: Life-Giving Groups 7

How Do We Make Disciples?
Learning Discipleship from Jesus
Jesus's Habits of Discipleship
We Are Relational Beings
The Challenge of Community

2. Principles: Rhythms of Life-Giving Groups 19

Why Our Rhythms Matter
Rhythm 1 — Word and Prayer: Connecting with God
Rhythm 2 — Fellowship: Connecting with One Another
Rhythm 3 — Hospitality: Connecting with Outsiders

3. Process: Multiplying Life-Giving Groups 35

The Language of Multiplication
Step 1: Discovering a Biblical Vision of Healthy Multiplication
Step 2: Setting Expectations for Healthy Multiplication
Step 3: Preparing for Healthy Multiplication
Step 4: Practicing Healthy Multiplication
Step 5: Maintaining Health After Multiplication

Conclusion 55

4. Practices: Appendices 57

    1. Leading Groups from 0 to 12
    2. The Five Rules of Community Groups
    3. Summer (and Liturgy) in Group Life
    4. Group Plan
    5. Rhythms Plan
    6. Creating Space: A Guide to Group Multiplication
    7. Multiplication Plan
    8. Neighborhood Plan
    9. Further Reading

Acknowledgments 97

About the Author 99

About Sojourn Network 101

Other "How-To" Books 103

SERIES PREFACE

Why should the Sojourn Network publish a "How-To" series?

It's an excellent question, since it leads to a more personal and pertinent question for you: *Why should you bother to read any of these books?*

Sojourn Network, the ministry I am honored to lead, exists to plant, grow, and multiply healthy networks, churches, and pastors. Therefore, it seems only natural to convert some of our leader's best thinking and practices into written material focusing on the "How-To" aspects of local church ministry and multiplication.

We love church planters and church planting. But we've come to believe it's not enough to do assessments and fund church plants. We must also help, equip, and learn from one another in order to be good shepherds and leaders. We must stir up one another to the good work of leading churches towards their most fruitful future.

That's why some books will lend themselves to soul calibration for ministry longevity, while others will examine the riggings of specific ministries or specialized mission. This is essential work to building ministries *that last*. But God has also placed it on our hearts to share our mistakes and most fruitful practices so that others might improve upon what we have done. This way, everyone wins.

If our prayer is answered, this series will bring thoughtful, pastoral, charitable, gospel-saturated, church-grounded, renewal-based "practice" to the rhythms of local church life and network collaboration.

May these "How-To" guides truly serve you. May they arm you with new ideas for greater leadership effectiveness. Finally, may they inspire you to love Jesus more and serve his people with grace-inspired gladness, in a ministry that passes the test of time.

Dave Harvey
President, Sojourn Network

INTRODUCTORY LETTER

Dear Church Leader,

I've been on a long journey with community groups and have arrived at a strong conviction: Community groups are *the* best place for us — as relational beings — to become mature disciples of Christ.

I have spent ten years leading and hosting community groups, including seven years of serving as a community pastor at Sojourn Community Church in Louisville. I've been to numerous small group conferences, listened to podcasts and interviews, and at one point, gathered a few interns to read and summarize every single book on small groups ever written. (It's only about 40 books.) After all this, I am more convinced than ever of this truth: There is simply no substitute for people to grow in Christ-likeness together than the trenches of a local church's small groups.[1]

---

[1] Small groups are called community groups in most of our Sojourn Network churches, so I'll use "community group" language throughout this book.

But consider your own experience: Perhaps my statement rings a bit hollow for you. How many community groups have you been a part of that were truly life-giving? How many times have you left thinking, "I am so blessed to have these people in my life"? Many of us have been in different forms of small groups and Bible studies throughout life, and if we're honest, we have walked away more acquainted with their challenges than their life-changing power.

Why Are Community Groups So Hard?

Community groups are hard. Let me count the ways:

1. Complexity: People are complex, of course, so it's not surprising that organizing and leading a small group of people could pose some difficulty.

2. Preconceived Notions: Most believers have participated in some type of small group — whether in the church, at school, or in the marketplace — and bring some preconceived notions of how the group should operate.

3. High Stakes: The stakes are even higher for new church plants. If groups are going well, the church is almost sure to succeed; if your groups are struggling, then the church will likely fail to thrive.

4. Catch-All Mentality: In most young churches, community groups expand to become a "catch-all" for everything the church wants to do — discipleship, leadership development, counseling, theological growth, and local mission. Doing just one is hard enough! Doing them all is a prescription for overwhelmed leaders.

5. Burn-Out: When leaders are also hosting the group in their homes, the commitment also includes hospitality and possibly meal preparation. Thus, the burnout rate of leaders is understandably higher than other volunteer ministries.

6. Multiplication: Even when a group is successful and grows to the capacity of the host home, a new challenge emerges: How do we multiply this group without damaging the types of relationships we've spent months encouraging, stewarding, and loving?

7. New Responsibilities: Similarly, when a church grows to about five to eight community groups, the lead pastor can no longer adequately provide oversight of each group, so another layer of leadership must be introduced, typically pulling some of the best group leaders out of their role into a new responsibility — leading leaders.

8. Lack of Training: Pastors are typically ill-equipped in small group ministry. Despite the high prevalence of groups across American churches, pastors can spend years in seminary and not hear a single lecture — let alone a whole course — on small groups.

Finally, with the blessings of growth come a new set of questions:

- Should we pay for childcare so parents can attend?
- Should we do sermon discussion or develop content?
- How do we integrate mercy and local mission into our groups?
- How much should groups provide for benevolence needs in their midst?

- How do we respond to chronically absent members?
- When do we hire "a groups guy"?
- Not to mention: What in the world do we do with teenagers?

This list isn't exhaustive, but we have enough complications to make the point: Community is messy.

Are Community Groups Worth It?

These challenges raise a logical question: Are community groups still worth it today?

Tim Keller's sentiment resonates deeply: "Small groups don't work at all, and we're totally committed to them!"

Despite these challenges, I now believe more than ever that the first sentence of this booklet is true: Community groups are the best place for us — as relational beings — to become mature disciples of Christ.

My goal and prayer is to show you a better way of doing community. This book will not remove every challenge nor answer every question. But it will call you to a biblical view of community and refresh your vision for discipleship in groups. Throughout this book, I'm pleading with you: *Pour your hearts and souls into your community groups.*

> **Community groups are the best place for us to become mature disciples of Christ.**

As a pastor or church leader, you will not regret a minute spent in prayer, reflection, or planning for your groups. If you can cultivate healthy, multiplying groups in the first five years of your church plant, you will reap decades of spiritual transformation and church health.

Let me repeat it again: *Pour your hearts and souls into your community groups.* Your investment in community groups will pay off exponentially in the souls of your people and the culture of your church. Community groups cannot be an afterthought.

This book aims to help you answer two questions for your context:

1. How will our community groups cultivate mature disciples of Jesus?
2. How will our community groups grow and multiply to sustain a healthy church?

Both questions will mean moving past seeing community groups as mere fellowship and Bible study. They must become the primary place of discipleship, which I define as *the life-giving way of being with Christ and becoming like him together.*

How to Use This Book

This book is designed for community group leaders, coaches, and pastors. My goal is to be as brief and helpful as possible, while still immersing you in biblical principles and best practices.

As a community group leader, you may want to take a few weeks to read through this entire booklet. You are welcome to read start-to-finish, or you may want to jump directly to the three rhythms of healthy groups (chapter two), the section on group multiplication (chapter three), or even the appendix, where there are eight short resources.

You may also want to read through sections of this guide with your community group. If you choose to do this, you could follow this schedule by having members read the chapters ahead and then meet to discuss.

Week 1 — Philosophy: Life-Giving Groups
Week 2 — Principles: Rhythms of Life-Giving Groups
Week 3 — Process: Multiplying Life-Giving Groups

If you are a pastor, community group coach, or ministry director, I hope this book is especially helpful for you. It's no easy responsibility to oversee community groups as a leader of leaders. My prayer for you is that these chapters re-engage your love of community and that the appendices provide you with practical resources for moving your ministry toward health and growth.

In some cases, you may have a different model of community groups, so I've tried to keep the emphasis on the biblical vision of community, broad principles for effective, life-giving groups, and a reasonable process for multiplying these groups for long-term health and growth. Again, you may find the appendices most helpful, and I expect each appendix will spur your imagination to create resources to fit your calling and context. Let's get started.

Grace and peace,
Jeremy Linneman

PHILOSOPHY

LIFE-GIVING GROUPS

What makes for a healthy community group? What must happen for a community group to become a primary place for transformation in a believer's life?

In this first chapter, I want to answer these questions by laying out a philosophy of life-giving groups.

I am assuming "life-giving groups" ministry is just one aspect of your church's overall vision of cultivating mature disciples of Jesus — as it should be. The problem, for many of our churches, is that our vision for groups is often divorced from our overall vision for discipleship.

Perhaps, then, the best question you can ask is: How will our community groups cultivate mature disciples of Jesus?

If Jesus commissioned us to *make disciples* of all nations (Matthew 28:19), our highest goal for community groups can't merely be fellowship or knowledge or visitor retention. Our goal must be mature disciples — men and women who are full of the life of Christ.

Making mature disciples is not just another "model" or program of small groups. Life-giving groups are those where members are:

1. Becoming fully mature disciples of Christ through the Word and prayer.
2. Joyfully doing life together with their group.
3. Regularly creating space for outsiders to enter and be known.

How Do We Make Disciples?

When discussing discipleship, many things may come to mind — a class, a program, a Bible study, family worship, one-on-one mentoring, a core set of doctrines, or an early developmental stage.

I've been in a group where accountability was king and pressed its members weekly (in gender-specific groups) to confess sins and recite scriptures. I've been in a "marathon" group regularly meeting for more than three hours a night — and we wondered why families with young children weren't sticking around. And I've even personally led a group naively assuming discipleship would just happen if we all hung out enough. (More on my mistakes later.)

Discipleship is the life-giving, grace-filled process of being with Christ and becoming like him

However, discipleship is not as difficult as the church has made it out to be, nor are there any magic bullets. Discipleship is neither a duty to perform nor a puzzle to solve. Discipleship is the life-giving, grace-filled process of being with Christ and becoming like him together.

First, discipleship will be *life-giving* if it is truly centered on Jesus Christ, he who is the Way, the Truth and the Life. Our groups should primarily be marked by life and not stagnation, joy and not defeat, encouragement and not gossip. In other words, discipleship must be "gospel-centered" — ministry rooted in Jesus and his gospel.

Second, discipleship is *grace-filled*, recognizing spiritual transformation comes through God's grace, not simply our effort. God's grace enables us to be with Christ, motivates us to be with him, and makes us become like him (Titus 2:11–13). We will fail frequently, but his grace sustains us along the way.

Third, discipleship is *a process*, not just a theory, class, program, or time of the week. Discipleship is similar to a worldview — it's a new way of *living*, with new habits and routines.

Fourth, discipleship is a process of *being with Christ*, not primarily a way of doing more for him or the church. The first invitation of discipleship is not to grow or change or even obey; it is simply to come to Jesus. He says initially "come, *follow* me" (Matthew 4:19), rather than "come and be changed."

Furthermore, the words of Matthew 11:28–30 demonstrate our Lord's heart for his disciples: "*Come to me, all you who are weary and burdened, and I will give you rest. Take my yoke upon you, for I am gentle and humble in heart, and you will find rest for your souls. For my yoke is easy and my burden is light.*"

Fifth, discipleship is a way of *becoming* like him. Once we have spent time in the *presence* of the King, we will gradually be transformed by the *power* of the King. Our growth in Christlikeness produces a real change, and our obedience becomes an *internal* desire rather than an external compulsion. We become what we behold, according to Paul in 2 Corinthians 3:18: "*And we all, who with unveiled faces contemplate the Lord's glory, are being transformed into his image with ever-increasing glory, which comes from the Lord, who is the Spirit.*"

Lastly, discipleship happens *together*. Our being and becoming like Christ is not an individual pursuit. It is deeply personal, yet it does not happen primarily in a "Jesus and me" context. Instead, the best possible place of spiritual transformation is the local church — and more specifically, in a small, regular, committed group of believers pursuing the same end.

> **Discipleship happens together.**

Learning Discipleship from Jesus

If we want to find a blueprint for discipleship, we must begin where all true discipleship should begin: with the earthly life and ministry of Jesus.

When Jesus wanted to make disciples, he began with a small, life-giving group of people.

What did that look like? Jesus's life and ministry turned the world upside down. The ministry of Jesus was like nothing before and nothing since. His touch healed the diseased and disabled; his voice calmed the seas; his tears raised the dead.

Similarly, when Jesus's disciples took over his ministry, the world shook at their presence. They may have been uneducated, common people, but they had been with Jesus (Acts 4:13).

So what was so utterly world changing? Jesus and his early followers overwhelmed their neighbors — the religious, the irreligious, the proud, and the broken — with an invitation to life at its deepest and fullest. The disciples' teaching exposed the deepest wants and need of both the Jews and Greeks alike. Then the disciples demonstrated how these wants and needs are fulfilled in the life and words of Christ.

For centuries, both the Israelites and the Greco-Romans had wrestled with life's biggest questions, though without much progress. The Israelites were focused on law and morality but became disconnected from God. The Greeks and Romans emphasized self-discovery and human flourishing, but lacked true knowledge of God and his Word. Both had elements of truth without its true source.[2]

The message of Jesus was revolutionary to both groups: he offered a right understanding of the law and promised forgiveness of sins, *and* he demonstrated the path to true fulfillment and flourishing. Jesus and his ways are not a religion detached from reality. The words and pattern of Jesus presented a lens of viewing the world that was at once more heavenly and more "earthly" than anything before it. In the words of the late author Dallas Willard,

---

[2] For more on this argument, see Jonathan T. Pennington, *The Sermon on the Mount and Human Flourishing: A Theological Commentary*, (Grand Rapids: Baker Academic, 2017).

The people initially impacted by that message generally concluded that they would be fools to disregard it. . . How life-giving it would be if their understanding of the gospel allowed them simply to say, "I will do [the law]! I will find out how. I will devote my life to it! This is the best strategy I ever heard of!" and then go off to their fellowship and its teachers, and into their daily life, to learn how to live in his kingdom as Jesus indicated was best.[3]

In other words, the way of Jesus and his disciples was entirely life-giving, and it was lived out in the daily rhythms of small communities.

Jesus's Habits of Discipleship

We can learn several key themes from Jesus's work in and through his disciples. What were his habits of fellowship?

Jesus identified his key people.

He had twelve disciples — not thirteen, not eleven. And once he was in a relationship with these folks, he didn't kick some out or upgrade to better ones. The twelve weren't picked for their potential or their past behavior. Jesus knew these men, and they devoted their lives to him. These were his people, for better or worse — ahem, Judas.

---

[3] Dallas Willard, *The Divine Conspiracy: Jesus' Master Class for Life, Participant's Guide*, (Grand Rapids: Zondervan, 2010), 7.

Jesus invited his people into every area of his life.

Jesus is rarely found without his friends in the gospels. They accompany him on ministry trips, they stay together, and he brings them along to family gatherings, religious events, and holiday parties. He wasn't always teaching, but he was always *training*. His whole life was a lesson in truth and grace.

Jesus ate with his people.

As Matthew 11:19 simply states, "The Son of Man came eating and drinking." Eating was Jesus's favorite form of fellowship. He ate with everyone — Pharisees, tax collectors, strangers, and crowds — but he always seems to include his closest followers in these meals. For Jesus, meals were about the acceptance and celebration of the *other* — and this is why the religious leaders were so enraged by them.

Jesus lived on mission with his people.

Jesus began his public ministry with the calling of the twelve disciples. His mission was to them and through them, forming a mission-in-relationship. Even in teaching and healing, he was in community and training others. Preaching about his kingdom (evangelism) wasn't a solitary effort; Jesus lived on mission with his people as proof of the kingdom he was building.

In our community groups, we would do well to pattern our fellowship rhythms after the life and ministry of Christ. What would it look like if we actually did this?

We Are Relational Beings

We are relational beings made in the image of the triune God. Thus our rhythms of life must recognize this central truth. Being in relationship is not a trendy tool of discipleship; it is essential.

If you think about it, Jesus was never *not* in relationship. He eternally existed in the loving fellowship of the Trinity — Father, Son, and Holy Spirit. He came into this world not from the heavens split-wide but rather from his mother's womb. He was born into a normal family. He spent his childhood and early adulthood in obscurity. Later, he started his ministry by inviting others to follow him. Even on the eve of his crucifixion, he gathered for a meal with his disciples and then led them out to pray with him in the garden of Gethsemane. Among his final breaths from the cross, he instructed his disciples to care for his mother.

On occasion, he left his disciples to pray in solitude, but in general, Jesus did everything with this ragtag bunch of guys. His life and mission remind us that even he refused to live life in isolation. If relationships have always been essential to Jesus, shouldn't they be for us as well?

Like Jesus, we exist for relationships. We are created in the image of this triune God. To be fully *human* means to live in *relationships*. If Jesus was the most "fully alive" human ever, it shouldn't surprise us that a person cannot become fully human without a community.[4] *Simply put, we are created for community.*

---

[4] Richard Plass and James Cofield, *The Relational Soul: Moving From False Self to Deep Connection*, (Downers Grove: InterVarsity Press, 2014), 9–22.

Contemporary life has confirmed this: More than any single need, like self-esteem or personal autonomy, human beings most fundamentally need a place to belong.[5] A person without a family or small group of friends will struggle throughout life and never become whole. We are inescapably relational beings.

The Challenge of Community

So if we are relational beings, created for community, why are relationships so hard? Beyond the simple reality that we are also sinful beings living in a broken world, what makes community so hard today?

We are busy, we are over-committed, and we live dis-integrated lives.

Our life moves quickly, and we find ourselves saying things like, "I'm so busy," or "Life's just crazy right now." And often we fall into the trap of saying, "It's just a busy *season*." But the seasons slip into years, our nominal relationships pile up, and we become an inch deep and a mile wide.

> **We are busy, we are over-committed, and we live dis-integrated lives.**

It's a symptom of our culture, but apparently it hasn't always been this way.

---

[5] Roy F. Baumeister and Mark R. Leary, "The Need to Belong: Desire for Interpersonal Attachments as a Fundamental Human Motivation," in *Psychological Bulletin* 1995, Vol. 117, No. 3, 497–529.

Relational Circles

In former generations, people used to belong to a few circles of people: family was one circle, work was another circle, and church was another circle. In all, a person had five or six total circles, and there was a good deal of overlap between them — maybe 100–200 individuals and almost everyone lived within walking distance.[6]

But today, just think of the circles we try to manage:

> Family in town
> Extended family out of town
> Work
> Church
> Neighbors
> Old high school friends
> College friends
> Former co-workers
> Hobbies
> Kids
> Social media

And there's very little overlap — each circle is a disconnected grouping of people with just one or two things in common. Not to mention many of these "circles" are actually multiple circles: most of us have multiple teams we sit on at work. Even each of our kids have one or more relational circles — school, youth sports, and so on. And

---

[6] For more on these ideas and research see Randy Frazee, *Making Room for Life: Trading Chaotic Lifestyles for Connected Relationships*, (Grand Rapids: Zondervan, 2004).

social media is like one ever-expanding and relatively-meaningless circle!

My wife and I were recently on a date and noticed the couple next to us. Their conversation drifted over to us, and apparently it was their dating anniversary. Yet the guy was on his phone almost the entire time — his face glowing from his screen in the dark restaurant. His girlfriend finished her meal about twenty minutes before him, and finally she just got out her phone too. (My wife and I don't use our phones on dates, we just use old school social media: *people watching*.)

But the overuse of smartphones isn't the primary problem; it's a symptom of something deeper. And it's not just that we're busy, though we are. The issue is our lives are increasingly *superficial*. Whereas former generations managed four to six interconnected circles, the average individual now manages 40–50 disconnected circles. Thus we carry the anxiety of managing relationships with 1,000–2,000 individuals. How could we possibly go deep with this many people, across this many circles, and how could we possibly feel like our life is simple, integrated, or even manageable? *Our entire culture is an inch deep and a mile wide.*

This is our culture. We are drowning in busyness and superficiality. How can we possibly build and enjoy life-giving community? Is it even possible? Given the cost, is it even worth it?

Close Relationships vs. More Relationships

I believe, because we are created for community, that human flourishing — growth in Christ and true joy — can only be found in tight, Christ-shaped relationships. You will never be as happy and fully human as the moments you are fully known in committed, close, Christ-centered community.

Think about it like this: No one gets to the end of their life and wishes they had a few dozen more superficial relationships. No one wishes they had served on one more board or spent an extra 100 hours in the car eating fast food while shuttling toddlers to organized soccer practices. Absolutely no one gets to the end of their life and says, "I should have just mindlessly plowed through more days and months and years."

> **No one gets to the end of their life and wishes they had a few dozen more superficial relationships.**

No, it's always: "I wish I had invested more quality time in the people closest to me: my spouse, my friends, my kids."

This thesis — and it's deeply biblical — is that one of the most important ways we can live meaningful and counter-cultural lives in this culture is by *simplifying* and *centering* our lives. *It's better to have deep relationships with a few than superficial relationships with a thousand.* How does this thesis transform the everyday practices of our community groups? In the next chapter, we'll look at why the routines of our community groups must match what we believe about community and discipleship. We'll also discover the four most important community group rhythms for producing mature Christian disciples.

PRINCIPLES

RHYTHMS OF LIFE-GIVING GROUPS

Let's start with a depressing reality: while the message of Jesus is clear, life-changing, and rooted in everyday life, it has largely become disconnected from American church experience. Why?

Of course, disobedience and rebellion have deep roots in our hearts. But could we also be missing the immense power and practicality of Christ for our moment-by-moment lives? I believe our vision of the new life with God is lacking, and as a tragic result, both Christians and churches are largely powerless.

What we need is two-fold: *We need a fresh vision of Christ and our life in him (discipleship),* and *we need practical habits to develop new behaviors and rhythms of life in the church to make discipleship stick.* To quote Willard again, "The really good news for humanity is that Jesus is now taking students in the master class of life."[1] We can do this!

---

[1] Dallas Willard, *The Divine Conspiracy: Jesus' Master Class for Life,* (San Francisco: Harper, 1998), vxii.

Why Our Rhythms Matter

In order to grow in our conformity to Christ, we need to embrace new rhythms of life. We need new habits.

As many researchers have shown, we can only develop new behaviors through the repetition of practices reinforcing those behaviors. To be a great musician, time must be spent studying sheet music and practicing chords. Often, a mentor is needed to make the most of practice — and a supportive community to provide encouragement and accountability.

We all have some vision of a better life. And our habits

Conformity to Christ requires embracing new rhythms of life. We need new habits.

reveal exactly where our desire lies. If we want to become like Christ, we have to set our eyes on him, create rhythms of life that reinforce that desire, and remove any old ways of life that work against our new vision.[2]

So what rhythms will best cultivate discipleship in Jesus? What habits can our community group embrace to spur one another toward conformity to Christ?

The three discipleship rhythms are: word and prayer, fellowship, and hospitality. To put it another way, to grow in Christ, we embrace the habits of:

1. Word and Prayer — connecting with God.
2. Fellowship — connecting with one another.
3. Hospitality — connecting with outsiders.

---

[2] For more see James K.A. Smith, *You Are What You Love: The Spiritual Power of Habit*, (Grand Rapids: Brazos Publishing, 2016).

In the first chapter, we saw how following Jesus's patterns will transform the way we do community groups and ensure that our discipleship is effective. These three rhythms — also discovered in the life and ministry of Jesus — give us the necessary habits to make disciples in our community groups. Like Stephen Covey's famous book *Seven Habits of Highly Effective People*, think of these as the "Three Habits of Highly Effective Community Groups."

Please hear this: The point is not whether you meet weekly or bi-weekly, or if you meet in a home or a coffee shop, or even if you discuss the Sunday sermon content weekly or monthly. But whatever form it takes, we encourage you to do life together, apply the scriptures, meet with God in prayer, and create space for outsiders.

How you contextualize these three practices is up to you. But in my experience, a community group that neglects one of these three rhythms will struggle to be and remain healthy and life-giving over time.

Rhythm 1: Word and Prayer — Connecting with God

When Jesus spoke, people listened. He didn't come to put an end to the Old Testament law but instead to "fulfill" it. He brought the law to completion in his life and into fruitfulness by rooting God's ways in the hearts of God's people. Therefore, it's vital for our community groups to actually learn together how to meditate on God's Word together. We must read Scripture devotionally together to better root God's Word in our hearts.

Devotional Scripture reading, or biblical meditation, has often been described as a middle road between reading and prayer. We engage our minds with God's Word, then the words of our prayer come from our heart as we express ourselves to the Father. Biblical meditation can increase communal fellowship with God and it promotes a treasuring of God's Word over merely expanding our knowledge.

Learning to Meditate Together

For centuries biblical meditation has been practiced both individually and communally — and we can restore this practice in our community groups today. The church fathers spoke of "descending with the mind into the heart" — a helpful phrase describing biblical meditation. Meditation engages the mind by focusing it on God's Word. In the midst of a thousand concerns and thoughts, it directs our minds to stillness on God's Word in his presence. Like a centripetal force, meditating on Scripture pulls us, slowly, inward toward the center of communion with God.

The best place to begin Scripture meditation — whether individually or in a group — is the Book of Psalms. We must remember the Psalms were written for congregational use; to be read aloud, sung aloud, and prayed aloud with others. As Eugene Peterson once noted, just as a farmer uses tools to cultivate the ground and produce crops, so we can use our prayers to stir up our hearts and become more like Christ. In other words, if our prayers are tools, the Psalms are our toolbox.[3] God has given us 150 rich, impassioned songs, and prayers for our devotional life. Unlike any other of the Bible's genres, the Psalms enable us to express ourselves, understand our own hearts, find perspective for our circumstances, give language to our emotions, and pray God's Word back to him.

> **If our prayers are tools, the Psalms are our toolbox.**

In our group prayer, we can pray the Psalms to our Father in a powerful way — together, we can descend with our minds into our hearts. Here are three recommendations for making the most of these prayers:

First Reading: Content and Meaning

Gather your group and introduce the topic of biblical meditation. Before beginning your reading and prayer time, ask the Lord to bless your time of reflection together.

In this first reading, read the psalm aloud. Since it was written to be read (or sung) aloud, there's likely a natural rhythm and flow to it. The first time through, get a feel for the psalm's content, and pause for a moment whenever you see the word *Selah*. After the first reading, take about five minutes to ask basic questions about the psalm's content and meaning. What is the psalm's original context? Is the psalmist primarily writing a private prayer or a congregational song? How would you put the message of the psalm into your own words?

---

[3] For more see Eugene H. Peterson, *Answering God: The Psalms as Tools for Prayer*, (San Francisco: HarperOne, 1991).

Second Reading: Application and Meditation

Remind one another that the goal of devotional reading is increased fellowship with God, not merely understanding the psalm. With a basic understanding of the psalm's content and meaning, now read the psalm aloud again, this time more slowly and with longer pauses. As one person reads the psalm, the rest of the group can follow along in their Bibles or simply close their eyes and listen. The goal is to absorb the psalmist's prayer as much as possible. When you reach a *Selah*, pause for a few moments and reflect silently on the previous stanza.

After this second reading, take 20 to 30 minutes to discuss the psalm's movements in a more personal way. How do you resonate with the psalmist's cries for help? Where do you see yourself similarly in need of God? What aspects of your life are driving you to seek refuge in the Father?

Praying Together: Descending into the Heart

After your discussion time, close with prayer together. An excellent exercise for our prayer lives is learning to reword a verse or two of a psalm and then praying that reworded verse(s) aloud. Take turns doing this, putting the most significant or applicable part of the psalm into your own words and praying it to our Father. Use the language of the psalm and add your own requests, praise, and prayer for others. This exercise will be awkward the first time or two, but don't get discouraged.

In our groups, we have found new life in this historical pattern. Slow, meditative reading of Scripture, heart-level discussion with application, and deep personal prayer has drawn us closer to God and to one another. Groups can practice this kind of Bible-based prayer with visitors and non-Christians present, so long as it's explained well. We've found that outsiders expect us to be doing spiritual things, and are refreshed by a group of people who long to be more deeply connected to God's presence.[4]

Prayer Together: Spiritual Community

Of course, prayer in community group doesn't always feel this majestic. In most community groups I've been a part of or led, prayer has become just a way of listing others' needs out loud to God. We try hard to summarize Frank's work situation, try not to be condescending as we pray for Jim and Amy's struggling marriage, and make sure we "lift up" Sue's second cousin's knee soreness. My goodness, this doesn't feel significant at all. So what's so important about praying together as a community group?

Think back to Jesus's life and ministry again. In his famous teaching on prayer in Matthew 6:5–15, it's important to note that the Lord's Prayer seems to be instructing us in a prayer that we could offer *together*: "*Our* Father… Give *us*… Forgive *us*… Lead *us*…" Prayer certainly can and should be practiced in private, but it's instructive that the pattern our Lord gives us in his most famous prayer is a *shared* prayer.

In the same way, our heavenly Father wants us to come to him *together* with our needs and problems. Following the

---

[4] A version of this section originally appeared as Jeremy Linneman, "Three Steps for Meditating on Scripture in Small Groups," *The Gospel Coalition*, September 28, 2015, www.thegospelcoalition.org/article/3-steps-for-meditating-on-scripture-in-small-groups.

pattern of the Lord's Prayer, we have the opportunity to pray for each other's needs and so intercede on their behalf. As we pray for others in their presence, they feel God's love and presence. Similarly, we can pray boldly together for God to advance his kingdom and then live that prayer by faith together.

Think about it: Where did you learn how to pray? You probably learned to pray from experiencing another person praying for you or watching those praying near you. I learned prayer from my father around the dinner table, from my earliest community group leader when we blessed dinner, from my wife when our sons have been sick, and from my fellow pastors when we have gathered to plead with God for renewal in our midst.

Praying together is an essential aspect of community life.

Praying together is an essential aspect of community life, and along with the other rhythms and practices, it enables a flourishing in our life with Christ.

Rhythm 2: Fellowship — Connecting with One Another

As Christians, we should recognize that discipleship should happen in community.

Remember, we will not be improving Jesus's process of growing disciples in community with one another. We can't do this alone. We need each other. We have been created in the image of a Trinitarian God — he has eternally existed in community. To be fully alive then, we must pursue Christ in the context of committed relationships. This is part of God's eternal plan for our growth.

If there is a fundamental need to have a place of belonging in our lives, then our community groups could be the primary place of Christian formation and maturation. *But it's not enough to just be in a community group; we have to do life together.*

The rhythm of fellowship is the habit of gathering together, welcoming one another into our lives, and genuinely caring for each other. Before we even open the scriptures, pray, or evangelize, we should join ourselves to a like-minded, Christ-centered community — if we want to follow Jesus's pattern.

Fellowship is the context for the other practices — Word and prayer, as well as hospitality. In my experience, a group that struggles with the rhythm of fellowship will likely struggle with the other two. But if a community group truly embraces life together, they will have a much better chance

> **Groups that struggles with the rhythm of fellowship will likely struggle with the other two.**

of seeing transformation through living the Word, meeting with God in prayer, and creating space for outsiders.

So what might this look like?

In my current community group, we gather every Wednesday evening and about one Saturday each month. But the group isn't a meeting time or place; we seek to be family first.

A typical month may look like this:

- First Wednesday: Meet at our house for fellowship, Scripture discussion, and prayer.

- Second Wednesday: Meet at our house to spend time together as a group.
- Third Wednesday: Meet at our house for fellowship, Scripture discussion, and prayer.
- Saturday: Go to a local park for a hike and then lunch together.
- Fourth Wednesday: Ladies meet at a local ice cream store for fellowship and accountability, men stay at our house and talk while playing with the kids.

This type of schedule fits our people well, and gives us the opportunities to build relationships and reach outsiders. For example, the second Wednesday would be the ideal time to invite a family from the neighborhood. Recently, at my middle son's fifth birthday, we invited our next-door neighbors (who also have young children) to celebrate with us. They had never accepted an invitation to visit our group previously, but our kid's birthday party was an easy first step for them. They have since joined us on other evenings and attended a Sunday gathering with us as well.

Rhythm 3: Hospitality — Connecting with Outsiders

When we look at the gospels, we discover that Jesus is the model of hospitality. Jesus's public ministry began with his miracle at Cana — turning jars of water into wine at a wedding. He spent his time eating with "sinners and tax collectors," receiving gifts from marginalized women, encouraging widows, playing with children, and attending all major cultural events and parties.

Even though he didn't own a home, *Jesus is the most hospitable man to ever live.* How is this possible?

Meals with Jesus

In the gospel of Luke, the author says, "The Son of Man came..." and how would we finish that question? Would we say, "The Son of Man came preaching and teaching"? Or perhaps, "healing and casting out demons"? Or maybe, "establishing his kingdom"?

Luke writes, "The Son of Man came *eating and drinking*" (Luke 7:34). Jesus seems to be eating

> **Even though he didn't own a home, Jesus is the most hospitable man to ever live.**

throughout all of the four gospel narratives. Consider examples from Luke alone. Jesus . . .

eats with tax collectors and sinners (Luke 5),
is anointed at in a home during a meal (Luke 7),
feeds five thousand people (Luke 9),
eats in the home of Mary and Martha (Luke 10),
condemns the Pharisees over a meal (Luke 11),
urges people to invite the poor to meals (Luke 14),
invites himself to dinner with Zacchaeus (Luke 19),
gathers his disciples for the Last Supper (Luke 22),
and, risen from the grave, requests fish (Luke 24).[5]

---

[5] Tim Chester, *A Meal with Jesus: Discovering Grace, Community and Mission Around the Table.* (Wheaton: Crossway, 2011), 13.

One commentator notes, "Jesus is either going to a meal, at a meal, or coming from a meal."[6] Jesus is literally eating his way through the gospels.

Jesus's meals are full of significance. Few acts are more expressive of friendship and acceptance than a shared meal. In every culture, meals are a form of hospitality — regardless of whose house you're at. In fact, our English word "companion" comes from two Latin words meaning "bread" and "together."[7] Why are Jesus's meals so significant? *Jesus's meals are physical demonstrations of the grace he offers to the outsider.*

Jesus creates space for outsiders and identifies with them by sharing a meal with them.

Creating Space for Outsiders

What is hospitality? It's the distinctly Christian practice of creating space for outsiders. Hospitality, in a biblical sense, includes creating space:

> in our homes for our brothers and sisters in Christ,
> in our schedules and hearts for non-Christians,
> in our groups for our neighbors and co-workers,
> in our lives for the poor and marginalized,
> and in our city for people to be broken and genuine.

Just as Christ came to us when we were outsiders, so also the Church can open its heart and doors to those who don't know him. Romans 15:17 captures the clear gospel imperative

---

[6] Robert J. Karris, *Eating Your Way through Luke's Gospel* (Collegeville, Minnesota: Order of Saint Benedict, 2006), 97.

[7] Chester, *A Meal with Jesus*, 10.

of hospitality, "Therefore welcome one another as Christ has welcomed you, for the glory of God." As one Christian author put it:

> In our world full of strangers, estranged from their own past, culture and country, from their neighbors, friends and family, from their deepest self and their God, we witness a painful search for a hospitable place where life can be lived without fear and where community can be found.... That is our vocation [as Christians]: to convert the enemy into the guest and to create the free and fearless space where brotherhood and sisterhood can be formed and fully experienced.[8]

Hospitality in Practice

Let's pause now and consider our own stories. At one point, we were all visitors to a church and didn't know more than a person or two. How might our lives be different at this point if no one had invited us in and given us a "place at the table"?

Every one of us has been the recipient of the hospitality of others, and now we extend that same hospitable spirit to the next generation of church visitors — and to our own neighbors, co-workers, and friends.

This vision of hospitality is more than mere entertaining of course. Entertaining — putting out our best food, showing off our home, and inviting our most attractive guests — puts

---

[8] Henri J. Nouwen, *Reaching Out*, (New York: Image Books Doubleday, 1975), 65–66.

the focus on us. Hospitality, on the other hand, puts the focus on another meal — the eternal feast.

Furthermore, meals serve us in several ways. They nourish us, slow us down, allow for conversation, and build bridges with others. But to think of it another way: Jesus's meals weren't just *for* something else. Rather, everything else — life, work, family, suffering, everything — was *for* a meal with Jesus. In other words, all of human history, from creation to the cross to the new creation, happened so that we might have eternal communion with Christ.[9]

When we invite our neighbors over for dinner, when we take time to join our co-workers for lunch or happy hour, or when we offer a cold drink to a stranger, we are demonstrating the grace of God to one another.

Summary

Let's imagine how these three rhythms can work together. The more we internalize God's Word and pray to him together, the closer we become to one another. And as we connect with one another and encourage one another with God's Word, we become so familiar with the grammar of the gospel it begins to permeate our language with outsiders in a natural way.[10]

Even if it's not a "Word and prayer night," we can still pray for one another. Even when non-Christians are visiting,

---

[9] Inspired by and gleaned from Chester, *A Meal with Jesus.*

[10] Inspired by and gleaned from Jeff Vanderstelt, *Gospel Fluency: Speaking the Truths of Jesus into the Everyday Stuff of Life*, (Wheaton: Crossway, 2017).

we don't have to change all of our rhythms. How you contextualize and practice these three rhythms depends entirely on your situation. These exact gatherings may not fit your people and context. You may not be able to meet weekly, or you might be able to do all three of the rhythms each week. Once you know your people and those whom you are trying to reach, then adapt your gathering times. But whatever your exact practices, if you embrace these three rhythms with intentionality, I've regularly seen a collection of strangers grow together to become a life-giving community group.

PROCESS

MULTIPLYING LIFE-GIVING GROUPS

The first community group I ever led was a struggle.

We had multiplied out from another group that was not entirely healthy. The multiplication process was a bit rushed, and our members didn't feel like the previous leaders had cared well for them. As brand-new leaders, only twenty-three years old, we over-corrected to the previous error by over-promising our group longevity without multiplication.

I remember telling the group at our first gathering, "You don't have to worry about multiplying. We'll build and maintain strong relationships here." Everyone smiled and nodded in approval. However, after about nine months, our group had grown to the capacity of our little living room, and I knew it was time to bring up the topic of multiplication again.

When I told our group very gently that we should consider multiplying to create space for new people, they revolted. I hadn't expected them to remember my early words about not multiplying. I said, "Well, of course, we need to multiply: There's no space here!" But they responded, "Why do we need more space? We should just close the group to outsiders. They can go to other groups!"

I suddenly realized my mistakes. I had not started the group with an expectation of multiplication, nor had I regularly reminded the members of the need to stay open to outsiders.

These errors were not minor. We then faced an uphill battle trying to shepherd the group through the conversation, and it took close to a year to get the group ready to multiply. I figured that once it was time to multiply or send out members to start a new group, we could take a few weeks to talk through it, and everything would work out. I was wrong.

As the years have passed, I have been able to lead or oversee dozens of healthy multiplications. Some were easy, and some were still slow and challenging. But I've discovered, through trial and error, a five-step process to cultivate a healthy group for multiplication. I truly believe that growth and multiplication are the results of a healthy group, and multiplication itself can be a healthy, life-giving process. Multiplying a group or sending members out to start a new one are never painless or simplistic endeavors. But this process has enabled dozens of fruitful multiplications and new groups.

> **Multiplying a group or sending members out to start a new one are never painless or simplistic endeavors.**

The Language of Multiplication

When you're talking with your community group or your leaders about multiplication, you'll want to choose your words carefully. Here's what I mean: Although multiplication is a straightforward concept, some will have negative preconceived notions about it.

I've often found that younger members and new churches — those who haven't been in community groups for many years — find multiplication life-giving and exciting for the first few years. If they experience some version of these five-steps for healthy multiplication, they're likely to have a positive experience.

But when a member has been in community groups long enough to have multiplied several times, it's common to feel an amount of "change fatigue." In a few years, they could have been in three groups, adapted to the styles of three different leaders, and built dozens of new relationships. Introverts like me will especially struggle with this. As group leaders and pastors, we need to respect people's desire for stability in community and not suppress these normal feelings.

There is no one-size-fits-all plan for starting new groups.

In these cases, when your members are saying they're weary from recent multiplications, you may want to change your plan and your language. For instance, maybe instead of directly multiplying a group of sixteen adults into two groups of eight, consider empowering a strong couple to lead and open the door to anyone who wants to form a new group.

Perhaps only five or six adults will "plant" the new group, but you've still accomplished the formation of a new group to reach more people. And you've allowed deep relationships to remain intact within the "sending" group.

Please understand that multiplication will always need to be a case-by-case basis. There is no one-size-fits-all plan for starting new groups. My best advice is to use a handful of strategies like regular multiplication, one group "sending" out another new group, and starting new groups from all new members. Especially if your church is in a season of numerical growth, you'll almost certainly need several paths to create new groups.

Your community group must understand that the goal of community is the Christ-shaped spiritual maturity of its members, not mere fellowship, fun, or friendship. The New Testament does not allow us to define fruitfulness simply by fellowship; we are called to make disciples (Matthew 28:19). And yet, at the same time, fellowship is an essential component of community group and deep relationships must be encouraged between our members.

So for community groups to be healthy, *multiplication must be done in a way the promotes member health*, not in a way that neglects it.

Here are five steps for healthy group multiplication:

Step 1: Discovering a Biblical Vision of Healthy
    Multiplication.
Step 2: Setting Expectations for Healthy
    Multiplication.
Step 3: Preparing for Healthy Multiplication.

Step 4: Practicing Healthy Multiplication.

Step 5: Maintaining Health After Multiplication.

Remember what we've covered so far. Our groups will be life-giving places of spiritual formation when centered on Jesus's way of discipleship (chapter one) and practicing the three rhythms of discipleship (chapter two).

Step 1: Discovering a Biblical Vision for Healthy Multiplication

Most of the scriptures come to us in the form of stories.

Everyone loves a good story. Think of a good story you've heard recently — maybe the birth of a child, the way an elderly married couple met many years ago, or something from a movie or book. Think of how the story drew you in: the characters, the scenes, the conflict, the movement of action, the plot rising to a surprising outcome, and some sort of resolution. The elements of a good story are often similar.

We are all, by nature, story-lovers, and story-tellers.

How did you respond to that story? Did you feel the impulse to go out and tell it to someone else? Did you find yourself re-living scenes or moments from the story?

There are two essential marks of a great story: *A great story draws you in* — into the character and the plot. And *a great story sends you out* — you immediately want to retell it.

We are all, by nature, story-lovers, and story-tellers. It's simply human nature to want to tell everyone when a close friend has a baby, when you've gotten a new job, or when you've seen a great movie. Stories are powerful because they tap into the richness of our human experience. When something *noteworthy* happens, our joy isn't complete until we "note" it to one another.

In other words, we are hard-wired to be "sent out" and to "speak out" when something truly amazing happens.

But it's not just human nature to be "drawn in" to a deeply significant experience and then to be "sent out" to tell others about it. This is a beautiful pattern woven into the fabric of the great biblical story of God making a new people.

Foundation 1: The Pattern of Mission

In Genesis 12, God speaks to Abram, draws him into an experience of his presence, and promises to make him a blessing to all the nations. The moment after God draws Abram in, God sends Abram out, "*Go,* leave your country and your people and *go* to the land I will show you" (Genesis 12:1).

In Exodus 3, Moses is a murderer running for his life when God appears to him in a burning bush. Moses falls on his face in worship. The Lord tells him, "I have heard the cry of my people... Now *go*: I am sending you to Pharaoh to bring my people out of Egypt" (Exodus 3:10).

In Acts 13, as the church in Antioch is praying, fasting, and worshiping one evening, God gives them a powerful experience of his presence. He draws them in and speaks by his Spirit: "Set apart Paul and Barnabas for me to *go* to where I have called you" (Acts 13:2).

This is God's pattern for mission: *He draws us in and sends us out.* He draws us in to *know* him, and he sends us out to *make him known.* The gospel comes to us in order to go through us.

In the call of Abram, the pattern is clear: *We are blessed to be a blessing.* Why does God reveal himself to us? Why does he draw us into his presence and move us to worship? Why does he surround us with loving community — as in Acts 13? God always blesses us so that we might be a blessing to others.

Now think of your own story: How has God revealed himself to you over your Christian life? How has he invited you into a deeper life with him through this church? How has this community group provided life-giving friendships in Christ? Certainly, we are a blessed people.

Too often in our community groups, we want the blessing to reach us but not move through us. Our members want to each be the last ones to join a group. No one wants to exclude others from a group, but once we are in, sometimes we want to close it off. As a result, we as community group leaders need to put the biblical vision of multiplication before our people regularly.

> **Too often, we want the blessing to reach us but not move through us.**

Foundation 2: Creating Space for Outsiders

Multiplication is a pattern throughout the Story of the Bible, but the apostle Paul gives us a second foundation for motivation: Christian hospitality — creating space for others — will naturally lead to multiplication.

Paul writes in Romans 12:9–13:

Love must be sincere. Hate what is evil; cling to what is good. Be devoted to one another in love. Honor one another above yourselves. Never be lacking in zeal, but keep your spiritual fervor, serving the Lord. Be joyful in hope, patient in affliction, faithful in prayer. Share with the Lord's people who are in need. Practice hospitality.

Remember the rhythm of hospitality. If our groups are regularly creating space for outsiders, growth will happen naturally, and new groups will be needed. The apostle Paul recognized the importance of hospitality for true community and sincere witness. What is hospitality? It's *the distinctly Christian practice of creating space for outsiders.*

Put yourself in the shoes of a visitor to your church: You don't know more than a person or two, but you want to get involved. Imagine if you were told that community groups were the way to get involved in the church, but unfortunately each group was currently closed. What message would that send?

Imagine instead showing up to church and immediately being invited to someone's community group. Imagine showing up to that group for the first time and seeing several smiling faces and plenty of open seats.

My experience suggests that first-time visitors community group will decide to join that group long-term within fifteen minutes of arriving. The decision, typically, is not based on curriculum or the demographics of other members in the group. First-time visitors join groups that are immediately hospitable to them.

Foundation 3: The Great Commission

> Then Jesus came to them and said, "All authority in
> heaven and on earth has been given to me. Therefore
> go and make disciples of all nations, baptizing them in
> the name of the Father and of the Son and of the Holy
> Spirit, and teaching them to obey everything I have
> commanded you. And surely I am with you always, to
> the very end of the age" (Matthew 28:19–20).

Just as Jesus spoke these words to his own twelve
disciples, so he is still speaking this commission to us today.
Here in this important charge, we discover the third and final
foundation for healthy group multiplication: *As Christ sends us,
he also goes with us.*

The Great Commission sends us to our neighborhoods,
our cities, our enemies, and the nations to make disciples.
What a huge task and responsibility! But Jesus doesn't send
us out to make him known until he has first drawn us in to
know him (the first foundation), and he doesn't send us out
ill-equipped.

In fact, Jesus doesn't even send us out alone; he promises
to go with us, "Surely I am with you always, to the very end
of the age." And according to Acts 1–2, Jesus is with us by
giving of the Holy Spirit. See, this is the full pattern: God first
draws us into his presence to dwell with him deeply, and then
he sends us out through Christ to make him known, but he
also goes *with* us by his Holy Spirit. From the first movement
to the last, God is with us — indeed, his name is "Immanuel"
(Matthew 1:28).

Launching a new group is no small task. Even sending some of your closest friends out to another group can be a difficult change. But we have to remember that, in starting a new community group to reach more people, we are both participating in and fulfilling Jesus's Great Commission!

Step 2: Setting Expectations for Healthy Multiplication

After establishing a biblical vision for open, multiplying groups, how do we ensure the ensuing multiplication process is healthy? How do we set proper expectations for multiplication?

I recommend explicitly setting expectations for a community group's multiplication.

1. Prioritize the Spiritual and Relational Health of the Members

Remember, our overall goal of community life is not the total number of groups we can launch and sustain over a period of time. The goal is the formation of disciples in the image of Christ.

Thus, if we neglect our members' spiritual and relational health during multiplication — which we have been investing in for months or years prior to multiplication — we can sour our members towards ever multiplying again and lose trust with our members on where our "real priorities" lie.

2. Remember that Multiplication Furthers Our Members' Spiritual and Relational Health

Teaching the three biblical foundations for multiplication is a great place to start. My "Creating Space: A Guide to Healthy Group Multiplication" appendix is a three-week discussion guide based on these foundations and includes discussion questions, guided prayers, and worksheets for your group. We must convince our members that multiplication is not an extra, but the biblical outflow of healthy life-giving groups.

3. Set a Multiplication Expectation at the First Gathering

Community group leaders must explicitly teach multiplication from the beginning of the group — not just before a needed multiplication. For example, when launching your first group, or as soon as a new group begins, the leaders need to give a vision for multiplication and a general timeline.

The leaders could say something like, "As we start this group, we want to remember that we are seeking not only our spiritual growth but also the spiritual growth of others. This is why we invite people into our group. When our group reaches about sixteen adults, and when new leaders are ready, we'll slowly multiply into two groups. We expect this will happen in about 12–24 months." You may even want to do this weekly or monthly when you review the rules of your community group (see appendix "The Five Rules of Community Group").

I remember when one of our groups at Sojourn had been together for three or four years without multiplying. There were more than twenty adult members and maybe a dozen kids, and more groups were needed across the congregation. But the leader had never brought up multiplication before this, and when he brought it up for the first time, fear and confusion and many tears rippled across the room. It took more than a year for this group to become ready — spiritually and relationally — to multiply.

4. Keep the Mission before the People

Group leaders should be continually reminding the members of our missionary identity in Christ. We should often see new people join our group — both from church and through relationships in the community. Experiencing growth firsthand will then help members grasp the need for creating space and multiplying.

5. Multiply When Leaders are Ready, Not When You Have Too Many People

I'm frequently asked, "At what number of people should we multiply?" But it's not the best metric to use for a multiplication timeline. A number of factors will determine how many adults and kids a group can have while remaining healthy and open to visitors. Some of our members' houses can accommodate twelve adults; others can handle thirty adults. Some of our groups will need to multiply once when about eight kids come regularly; others can have twenty or more kids and not run into too much trouble.

But still, the number of people should not be *the* determining factor in when you multiply. Nothing is more important than your leaders' readiness.

A group can be too big or too small, but with the right leaders, it will remain healthy and growing. As soon as new leaders are identified, trained, and ready, a new group can be deployed. Typically, six adults are enough to start a new group — a leading couple and four other adults.

Step 3: Preparing for Healthy Multiplication

Multiply into Different Neighborhoods When Possible

There should be an expectation that we are on mission to our neighbors, and thus multiplication will occur in a way where two new groups can more effectively reach their neighbors.

A couple of years ago, the community group my wife and I were leading reached about twenty adults. We had already identified another couple who would lead the second group and had communicated openly with our members. They felt the pressure of trying to gather in our small home, understood that we existed to invite others in, and were ready to multiply. So how did we decide which individuals and families would go to which group?

In our case, a major road ran through the area where our members were living. We realized that almost exactly half of our members lived west of the road, and the rest lived east of it. We pitched the idea to the group of splitting along this geographical line to focus more specifically on our neighborhoods. We gave each member the option to ask to go to a different group, but each member liked the plan, and it was so.

Set a Balanced, Realistic Multiplication Timeline

As a group leader who has experienced numerous group multiplications, I tend to want to multiply more quickly than others. Once new leaders are ready and there are six adults to form the group, I could say a prayer and send them off with a blessing. But most members will experience this as a rushed group "split." Most of our members will need to move more slowly and have explanations discussed openly.

When it comes to the "multiplication timeline," this is my general rule of thumb: it should seem a bit too slow for the leaders and a bit too quick for the members. In this way, it stretches the leaders to be patient and do the hard work of preparing people to multiply well. But it also stretches the members to multiply before they're 100 percent ready, thus having to trust God for the process.

> **The "multiplication timeline" should seem a bit too slow for leaders and a bit too quick for members.**

Let Members Choose Their Group

In the past, one of the mistakes I've made as a leader is to try to figure out which people should go with which group, and try to steer people in those directions. Instead, I think it's a much better practice to set two options in front of your members and let them choose. Do they want to go with the new group or stay with the sending group? The church is a voluntary organization, and we should be quick to empower our people to make their own decisions — especially regarding where they'll spend this important discipleship time each week.

Step 4: Practicing Healthy Multiplication

Throw a Multiplication Party

When it's finally time to multiply, gather everyone from the original group to throw a party. It should feel more like a graduation than a funeral. Gather in the backyard, cook a meal together, or host a movie night for the kids. Do something that celebrates the successful multiplication of one community of believers into two. You may even want to take time for members to share how the group was instrumental in their spiritual journey. Or you can just party.

Commission the New Leaders Publicly

This is one of the best ways to honor and bless community group leaders, and it also generates excitement and exposure for groups in general. Bring your new leaders up front at a Sunday worship service, and commission them to their new ministry. You may bring up the sending leaders as well, or have all the elders up front to lay hands on them. You can give the new leaders a gift — a Bible and a journal or a bunch of pasta and sauce to make together as a group that week — and encourage the congregation to applaud the leaders' sacrificial service to the church. This communication of authority and value will be powerful in your church.

Set Ground Rules for the New Group

See the appendix: "The Five Rules of Community Group." For the first few weeks, you may want to read these rules out loud, a la Fight Club. Once your group understands the rules, you won't have to revisit them every week, but your members will be able to remind one another of simple rules like, "Hey, remember we 'Put Others First,' so let's give her a chance to speak."

Start the New Group with a Renewed Vision

Once your new group starts — and both groups may want to do this — you may want to start a short series together to gain a renewed vision. A short study discussing the four discipleship rhythms would help set a vision and direction for the group. Maybe you want to spend six weeks on the six chapters of Ephesians and discuss how your group will seek to grow together and reach others.

Whatever your vision of group life is, it's ideal to revisit that vision with each new group multiplication. If your groups are multiplying every one or two years, it becomes a helpful reminder for all leaders and members. You don't want multiplications to feel like high school breakups. Each new group is a celebration to remind both the new and the sending group of the biblical foundations for multiplication.

Jump Quickly into Mission as a New Group

Especially for a group meeting in a new location, there is no better time to start evangelistic efforts as a group. If the new group is meeting in an apartment or home for the first time, the group can spend one of the first gatherings going out and inviting people from the neighborhood. Consider setting a fun, family-style gathering about a month or two into the new group, and specifically invite neighbors to that low-pressure gathering.

Your neighbors' first experience of your community group shouldn't be the parking issues created! As soon as you start your group, reach out to them, share your vision for community with them, and invite them to join you!

So once you've started your new group, how do you maintain health over the long haul?

Step 5: Maintaining Health After Multiplication

I've found a few final things to be helpful in maintaining health after group multiplication.

Gather Two or Three More Times with Both Groups

About a month after the multiplication, then maybe again in 3–6 months, gather both groups together for a meal or outdoor party. This is a great way to reconnect with one another, meet new visitors that have joined since the multiplication, and hear stories from the new groups. These post-multiplication gatherings help remind us that multiplication can be done well, relationships don't fall apart overnight, and new groups can create space for new people to experience Christ and community.

Form a Coaching Region Where Groups Still Share a Common Mission

In an ideal situation, establish a geographically based coaching region for groups that have recently multiplied. For example, if you have a group meeting on the south side of town, and it multiplies into southwest and southeast neighborhoods, you can have one elder or coach oversee the region.

When you reach 12–15 groups, it's ideal to have three or four regions of groups, each with its own pastoral or coaching oversight. At that point, three or four groups in the same region can gather for missional events and fellowship, helping the church to feel smaller while growing larger. This is also a strategic step in getting pastors and members working together to reach a very particular part of the city.

Give Multiplication Testimonies at New Group Leader Training

Once a church has more than a dozen groups, you'll likely need to add a formal group leader training component (if not sooner). During these trainings, make sure to give examples of healthy multiplication. These testimonies can come from the leaders or even the group members. Let group leaders ask questions like: "What has worked best? What was your timeline? What would you do differently?"

The long-term health of your community group ministry depends significantly on the health of each group's multiplications. And healthy multiplication is possible by setting a robust vision, reasonable expectations, with proper preparations for each new group, and continuing to care for the people in and through the multiplication process. When these elements are in place, you will likely see a slow, steady increase of new groups.

CONCLUSION

We began this book by making a strong claim: Community groups are *the* best place for us — as relational beings — to become mature disciples of Christ.

Launching and multiplying life-giving groups is not for the faint of heart. But there is simply no substitute for people to grow in Christ-likeness together than the trenches of a local church's community groups.

I hope and pray these brief chapters encourage you to unleash the life-changing power of your community groups. Again, I want to exhort you: *Pour your hearts and souls into your community groups.* Your investment in community groups will pay off exponentially in the souls of your people and the culture of your church.

> **Launching and multiplying life-giving groups is not for the faint of heart.**

In the appendices that follow, you'll find several resources designed for pastors and ministry overseers to help provide your community group ministry with structure. You may be able to put them immediately into use, or you may want to use the principles and ideas to create your own resources.

My prayer for you is the same as Paul's for the Ephesian church. Through your community groups:

Now to him who is able to do immeasurably more than all we ask or imagine, according to his power that is at work within us, to him be glory in the church and in Christ Jesus throughout all generations, for ever and ever! Amen (Ephesians 3:20–21).

PRACTICES

APPENDICES

APPENDIX ONE

LEADING GROUPS FROM 0 TO 12

In church planting contexts, community groups can be the best way to reach the unchurched, build strong community, and identify future leaders.

Having led in the early years of three new congregations, I recommend a general process for planting healthy groups in a new church environment. If you are planting groups from the beginning — which I encourage — then your community groups will each serve as a microcosm of the church as a whole for the first few years.

Starting your first few community groups with strength will enable a healthy trajectory for your new congregation, while neglecting these groups can be costly to the whole church. While every context is different, I encourage some broad principles and practices.

Launching the Pilot Group

Since the first community group will be a microcosm of the church plant, it's typically best for the lead pastor and his wife to lead the pilot group. The group doesn't necessarily have to be hosted in the lead pastor's home, but setting the culture is crucial as it will be likely replicated dozens of times in the coming years. This pilot group can turn into a core group or launch team, and your future leaders may come from this group as well.

The lead pastor typically sets the tone and culture of the church from this early community group. It's almost impossible to overstate the importance of the lead pastor's vision for the pilot group. Most church planting statistics show that people who join a new church do so for the community. Whereas a church of 200–400 will grow largely through visitors attracted to the preaching and worship, churches under 200 tend to grow by fostering deep community through engaging community groups.[1]

Thus the pilot community group should get a large amount of the church planter's best energy. This will be difficult for some. Whereas most church planters are trained in biblical studies, preaching, leadership, and mission, few have received significant training in community groups. As a result, the typical church planter overestimates the need to

---

[1] For church size and growth dynamics, see Timothy J. Keller, "Leadership and Church Size Dynamics," *Gospel in Life*, March 2, 2010. www.gospelinlife.com/leadership-and-church-size-dynamics.

See also Bill Easum and Bill Tenny-Trittian, *Effective Staffing for Vital Churches*, (Baker Publishing, 2012).

teach and cast vision and underestimates the need to build relationships and deploy members for mission.

The most effective church planters I've witnessed typically do a few things well. They often:

- Gather in another member's home and train the hosts as future leaders.
- Share a meal together with the group (approximately 30–60 minutes of group time).
- Lead a short Bible study or devotional that blends prepared teaching with well-planned questions and times of discussion (30–60 minutes).
- Offer childcare for families with young children, perhaps using a children's ministry curriculum.
- Spend a generous amount of time sharing life updates (15–30 minutes).
- Prepare the group for regular growth and multiplication.
- Gather the group outside of regular meeting times for increased fellowship.
- Allow significant time for prayer weekly (15–30 minutes).

Consider meeting on Sunday evenings prior to launching your first Sunday gatherings. This will give you the opportunity to launch Sunday evening services if needed, or the community could remain a Sunday evening group if you start morning services. You may also want to have a musician lead a few worship songs at the beginning of the gathering time, although you'll need to subtract this time from discussion, sharing, and prayer. In total, two hours seems to be a good maximum gathering time.

The First Multiplication

Hopefully, this pilot community group will reach new people and grow to be multiplication ready. As described in chapter three, the leader must lay out a vision for multiplication from the first gathering to increase the likelihood of a healthy new group in the future.

Ideally, the next community group leaders after the planter's family will have some experience leading a small group. Being the first non-pastor community group leader is a big responsibility, and many people may not want to step into this role. While you certainly want a very capable leader and high-character person in this role, you will also need to trust God with the people he has given you.

In my opinion, the two non-negotiable things to look for in a group leader at this stage are character and relational skills. While some leadership background and theological knowledge will be helpful, those can also be provided through training over time.

While the need for a character-qualified leader or couple should be obvious, we can often forget to look for strong relational skills in our leaders. Remember, your church of 20 to 40 adults will grow primarily from life-giving relationships, not vision and doctrine. Although God can use anyone to build his church, it is typically not wise to entrust this particular role to individuals who lack social awareness or who aren't relationally oriented.

As for the process of multiplication, following chapter three should help ensure a healthy new group. You do not want to rush this first multiplication. This multiplication will set the DNA for future multiplications and you must prayerfully seek to make it as healthy as possible.

Barriers to Growth

In leading groups and coaching numerous other pastors and leaders, I've noticed some common growth barriers for groups ministries. You may be familiar with growth barriers for church attendance; there are similar barriers to group ministries. I would expect to see occasional slowing of multiplication at the following points:

5–6 groups: At this stage, the lead pastor will be unable to oversee each community group adequately; it's ideal to identify another elder or leader who can come alongside him and coach these growing groups toward health.

10–12 groups: At this stage, you want to consider having three to four coaches overseeing 3–4 groups each. The lead pastor will need to consider focusing his time on equipping group coaches and training leaders to serve the whole. Monthly or quarterly gatherings of all the leaders together will help with vision renewal and equipping as well.

25–30 groups: While not all churches will reach this number of groups, for many this will be another difficult barrier. In fact, I have talked to multiple churches over 1000 in attendance that can't get past this number of groups despite consistent Sunday growth. At this stage, the lead pastor is typically unable to oversee the number of coaches needed, and even then, a second layer of leaders coaching coaches is ideal. In other words, to grow beyond 30 groups, a church will typically need a full-time groups pastor or leader, plus three or four committed lay elders or head coaches overseeing three or four coaches each. This becomes a highly-structured ministry, so keeping a personal touch from the pastoral team to the group leaders is indispensable. Here, monthly group leader gatherings are essential, and a quarterly or annual new group leader training should be considered.

While you may be thinking, "We'll never reach 30 groups!" You still want to plan for it. Even if your growth is slow or if your groups have plateaued, it's still helpful to keep training apprentices to be leaders, leaders to be coaches, and coaches to be elders and ministry overseers. You will never regret having a surplus of well-trained, experienced, and relationally oriented leaders in your church.

Coaching Structures

In general, you will want to have a coach for every three or four community groups and an elder or head coach for every 10–12 groups. Just like with multiplying, these are conversations to have long before the need is urgent.

Some great group leaders won't enjoy or be effective at coaching. Others may be average group leaders but incredible coaches. It's often hard to "promote" a leader to a coaching position and then remove them later. What is the alternative?

In many of the groups I have overseen, the best-case scenario is gradually working group leaders into coaching responsibilities. Give them a no-commitment trial period. For example, if a leader couple has successfully multiplied two groups, the pastors should consider giving them coaching oversight of the new group while still leading their own. After six months of coaching just one group, they may decide it's not for them and hand the group to another coach — no messy removal needed. On the other hand, they may enjoy it so much that the pastors give them two or three other groups and have them step out of their group leadership role. Either way, it's a good training ground and minimizes damage.

As a church or region grows to 10–12 groups, you may also want to identify a leader or member to take primary responsibility for pastoral care and counseling needs. While we can all shepherd one another, having a dedicated counseling volunteer for every 10–12 groups will enable your group leaders to remain primarily focused on group health and multiplication.

APPENDIX TWO

THE FIVE RULES OF COMMUNITY GROUP

To better facilitate depth and trust among your participants, consider reading aloud through the Five Rules before your discussion and prayer time. These guidelines can also guide your ongoing relationships with your group — since only a portion of your life together as a group will be in discussion and prayer.

1. We Come As We Are

We are not perfect people, and we all need a safe place to gather and be who we are. Community groups are that safe place. What is said here stays here, and we do not gossip about information outside this group. **However, if someone shares something that endangers him/herself or others, or if there are legal implications, the leader will share information with a pastor.

2. We Put Others First

We are here to serve and love one another, not simply to receive care ourselves. We all participate in the discussion either as active listeners or speakers. We each keep our sharing to 3–5 minutes each, and remain actively engaged as others are speaking.

3. We Encourage and Comfort

In Christ, we have the power to be present with the fullness of the Spirit's presence within us. We acknowledge that we can't fix or change one another, so we instead promise to provide encouragement and comfort. We don't express judgment or disgust toward one another's struggles. And we don't give unwarranted advice! When we want to give additional counsel, we ask permission after the gathered time.

4. We Journey Together

We are relational beings, created in the image of a Triune God. Because we are created for community, we need each other to grow in Christlikeness. We invite one another into our journey and walk through life together, following up with one another throughout the week. Because God never gives up on us or leaves us alone, we commit to journeying with one another through thick and thin.

5. We Focus on Christ

We don't get side tracked by unhelpful issues in sports, politics, pop culture, and so on. In some cases, we can engage cultural issues from a Christ-centered perspective, but typically we delay these discussions until discussion time is over. We focus instead on Christ, the Word of God made flesh, because he alone is the Way, the Truth, and the Life. We cannot change one another or even ourselves; only Christ can bring about grace, truth, and healing by his presence.

APPENDIX THREE

SUMMER (AND LITURGY) IN
GROUP LIFE

Each year around summertime, community group leaders begin to ask, "What should we do this summer?"

Many groups choose to take a break from regular gatherings; other groups press on with their regular rhythms all summer; still, others find some reduced meeting schedule to work best for them. What is ideal for your group?

Remember There Is Freedom

Remember, your group is not a weekly gathering; it's a community centered on Christ — it's a people, not an event. So however you meet, whether regularly or irregularly, you're still a community group. No, you don't have to meet every week — especially as you'll have members and families traveling and managing sports schedules.

But as a community of friends and fellow Sojourners, I've always believed that the summer months are the best opportunities to build relationships with one another and share life with our neighbors. It would be a shame to "take off" all summer!

Find New Rhythms of Relationships and Renewal

In Louisville, the summer is a time of reduced responsibilities and increased family and recreation time. Even individuals and families without children seem to operate on a school year calendar. Over the nine years we lived there, my wife and I led groups and loved the summer months as a time to gather out back, cook dinner together, gather at Cherokee park or take a Saturday trip to Red River Gorge.

We typically spend far less time in the living room and much more time outdoors. It's just a great time to do "life together." Does one of your families have a busy sports schedule? The whole group could join them at a baseball game, cheering on their kids from the stands. Their kids will LOVE this! Remember too, you can celebrate birthdays, anniversaries, and basically anything: Find an excuse to bake a cake and hang out, and make it happen.

Join Your Neighbors on Their Turf

Our neighbors in the city use their summers going to farmer's markets, spending extra time in their gardens, and staying up late hanging out on front and back porches. We Sojourners can meet them on their turf. Consider taking your group out to one of the common spaces in your community: a park, play-ground, or forest. Louisville is a great place to connect around natural beauty: Waterfront Park, and amazing parks like Cherokee, Seneca, Iroquois, Jefferson Memorial, Tom Sawyer, and Bernheim. There are also many art fairs, barbecue contests, and outdoor concerts — as well as team recreational sports and community clean up events you can participate in together.

Study, Pray, and Enjoy the Life of the Spirit

Since the resurrection and ascension of Christ, the church has observed a traditional calendar year to practice the good news. At Advent, we long for Christ's appearance; at Christmas, we celebrate his birth and life; at Epiphany (January), we feast and live in Christ's power; at Lent, we practice repentance and lament; at Easter, we celebrate New Life; and after Pentecost (post-Easter), we experience the Holy Spirit and then practice ordinary time.

Ordinary Time begins with the celebration of Pentecost Sunday, when the Spirit descended with power on the early church and moved its members to worship and mission (Acts 2:1–13). In response to the good news about Christ (Acts 2:14–40), these Christians re-oriented their lives around one another — to the study of God's Word in community, to eating and drinking together, to providing for one another, to regular worship, and to sharing Christ with their neighbors together (Acts 2:41–47).

In ordinary time, approximately mid-May through mid-November, we especially remember three biblical themes:

1. God's saving action in history (the gospel), through our regular Sunday worship and the study of his Word in community.
2. The renewing experience of the Holy Spirit through our prayer, fellowship and evangelism.
3. The anticipation of a new heavens and earth, where everything sad comes untrue and his praise never ends.

Summer — part of the historical season of ordinary time — is our best opportunity to re-orient ourselves around the truth of God's Word, the fellowship of God's People, and the glories of God's World.

Take some time this week in your groups to discuss how you might make the most of this summer. What new rhythms could you cultivate? How can you celebrate? Which community spaces can you enjoy together? How can you let the Holy Spirit unite your hearts together and work through you to invite your neighbors into fellowship with Christ?

Have fun this summer![1]

---

[1] A version of this article was originally published by Sojourn Community Church, 2011, at sojournchurch.com/summer-in-group-life/.

APPENDIX FOUR

GROUP PLAN

This appendix is adapted from Brad House, *Community: Taking Your Small Group Off Life Support*.

Information

Region/Neighborhood: _____

Pastor/Deacon (Coach): _____

Leaders: _____

Hosts: _____

Apprentices: _____

Goals and Projections

Culture or people group focus: _____

_____

Names people that our group is praying will come to Christ this year through the group:

_____

_____

_____

_____

_____

Number of groups we want to see replicated this year to reach more people in our neighborhoods: _____

Opportunities

Participation (Building Relationships): _____

_____

Service (Loving the City): _____

_____

Hospitality (Invitation to Community): _____

_____

Fellowship (Prayer, Bible, Confession, Repentance, etc.): ____

_____

_____

APPENDIX FIVE

GROUP RHYTHMS PLAN

Information

Region/Neighborhood: _____

Pastor/Deacon (Coach): _____

Leaders: _____

Hosts: _____

Apprentices: _____

Rhythm 1: Word & Prayer

Rhythm 2: Fellowship

Rhythm 3: Hospitality

Annual Rhythms

Spring: _____

_____

Summer: _____

_____

Fall: _____

_____

Winter: _____

_____

APPENDIX SIX

CREATING SPACE: A GUIDE FOR GROUP MULTIPLICATION

Week One: Blessed to Be a Blessing

Read

Genesis 12:1–9

Big Idea

God draws us in to send us out. We are blessed to be a blessing.

Discuss

What fears do you have as our community group prepares to multiply? How might this go poorly?

Read

Read the section entitled "The Pattern of Mission" under "Step 1: Discovering a Biblical Vision for Healthy Multiplication" in chapter three.

Respond

How have you experienced the blessing of the Lord during your time in this community group? What has been most life-giving to you?

Consider those that have joined your group in recent weeks and months. Take a moment to encourage one another in how you've seen Christ and maturity growing in them.

It's never easy to multiply a group. In fact, if we love one another, it should be quite hard! Yet how do you envision this group blessing others by creating space for them to experience God and community?

Re-visit the first question. How do you consider your fears in light of the biblical pattern of blessing?

Apply

For the next seven days, commit to praying for this group multiplication every day. Pray for new leaders to emerge and be equipped. Pray for a host home or apartment to be offered. Pray for the process of sending out some of your own friends to be a blessing to their neighbors in a new group.

Next Week

We will continue discussing multiplication together by looking at the biblical theme of hospitality — the practice of creating space for others to encounter Christ and his community.

Pray

Let's pray together now that the Father would soften our hearts toward his pattern of mission and toward those who have yet to experience him. Pray that this group multiplication would serve to move us to embrace a more outward-facing lifestyle. Pray also that this process would enable others in this neighborhood to encounter Christ, the church, and the members of this great community.

Week Two: Hospitality as Mission

Read

Romans 12:9–13

Big Idea

Group multiplication is a means of Christian hospitality — creating space for others.

Review

Last week, we read Genesis 12 and discussed the pattern of mission: "God draws us in to send us out. We are blessed to be a blessing." The experiences of Abraham, Moses, Peter, Mary Magdalene, and the early church all testify: when God draws us in to know him, he then sends us out to make him known. It is a privilege to join God and the mission of the church by creating space in our lives and groups.

Read

Read the section entitled "Creating Space for Others" under "Step 1: Discovering a Biblical Vision for Healthy Multiplication" in chapter three.

Respond

Who was it that first invited you to this community group — or to your first group at this church?

If you have been through a group multiplication before, share what was positive and negative about it. What suggestions and reminders do you have for the group as we prepare to multiply?

Pray

First, let's pray together that our Father would strengthen our relationships even as we multiply groups. And let's also pray that the Father would soften our hearts toward those currently outside his church, move us to embrace a more outward-facing lifestyle, and enable us to "practice hospitality" in this neighborhood.

Apply

Take 15–20 minutes to begin the appendix Group Multiplication Plan *for the new group*. Fill out the Information at the top, discussing any decisions must be made.

Read and discuss the four goals of multiplication.

Discuss the first question under "Multiplication Vision." Specifically, who are you creating space for? Write out the names of friends, co-workers, and neighbors you might invite into the new or sending group.

Next Week

Next week, we'll read and discuss the Great Commission and finish the Community Group Plan. We'll also plan our final gathering (2 weeks from now): a big celebration party!

Week Three: The Great Commission

Read

Matthew 28:16–20 and Acts 1:1–11

Big Idea

As Christ sends us, he also goes with us.

Review

First, we discussed Genesis 12 and the pattern of mission: *God draws us in to send us out. We are blessed to be a blessing.* The experiences of Abraham, Moses, Simon Peter, Mary Magdalene, and the early church all testify: When God draws us in to know him, he then sends us out to make him known. It is, then, a privilege to join God and the mission of the church by creating space in our lives and groups.

Last week, we read Romans 12 and considered biblical hospitality — the distinctly Christian practice of *creating space for outsiders.* By multiplying our group, we are making room for new church members and our disconnected friends, neighbors, and co-workers.

Read

Read the section entitled "The Great Commission" under "Step 1: Discovering a Biblical Vision for Healthy Multiplication" in chapter three.

Respond

How have you specifically seen God invite us into and fulfill the Great Commission through this group over the months or years?

How do you now see God fulfilling the Great Commission through our group's multiplication?

How does it change your perspective that God — Father, Son, and Holy Spirit — is intimately involved in the sending and starting of this new group? How does his ongoing presence with us change this process?

As we move closer toward our last gathering, what final questions, fears or reservations do you have?

Pray

Let's pray together (as we have the last two weeks) that our Father would strengthen our relationships even as we multiply groups. Let's also pray that the Father would soften our hearts toward his Great Commission and those currently outside his church, and make us a more outward-facing and hospitable people.

Apply

Take 15–20 minutes to finish Group Multiplication Plan (at the end of this guide) *for the new group*. Read and discuss through the four goals of multiplication again, and review the progress you made last week. Complete any final questions remaining.

APPENDIX SEVEN

GROUP MULTIPLICATION PLAN

Let's pray together (as we have the last two weeks) that our Father would strengthen our relationships even as we multiply groups. Let's also pray that the Father would soften our hearts toward his Great Commission and those currently outside his church, and make us a more outward-facing and hospitable people.

Take 15–20 minutes to finish Group Multiplication Plan (at the end of this guide) *for the new group*. Read and discuss the four goals of multiplication again, and review the progress you made last week. Complete any final questions remaining.

Next, confirm and write out the names of who will be committing to each group, and pray for one another.

Sending (Original) Group:

Leaders: _____

Hosts: _____

Apprentices: _____

Members: _____

_____

_____

_____

_____

_____

New Group:

Leaders: _____

Hosts: _____

Apprentices: _____

Members: _____

_____

_____

_____

_____

_____

Next Week

Our next gathering — a celebration of the multiplication will be on: _____

_____

Then, our first week of meeting as two community groups will be: _____

_____

Lastly, we will get back together as two groups on the following dates for fellowship: _____

_____

_____

_____

APPENDIX EIGHT

NEIGHBORHOOD PLAN

This appendix is adapted from Brad House, *Community: Taking Your Small Group Off Life Support.*

Information

Neighborhood: _____

Pastor/Deacon (Coach): _____

Number of Groups in Our Neighborhood: _____

Resources

Locations of Natural Community: _____

Service and Event Agencies: _____

Local Papers and Newsletters: _____

Goals

Vision for Our Neighborhood: _____

How many people are we praying to see come to Christ through community groups in the next year? _____

Number of groups currently in our neighborhood: _____

Projected number of groups in:

    3 Months: _____

    6 Months: _____

    12 Months: _____

How many apprentices or new leaders do we need in the next year? _____

APPENDIX NINE

FURTHER READING

Discipleship in Community

Dallas Willard, *The Divine Conspiracy* & *Renovation of the Heart*
James C. Wilhoit, *Spiritual Formation as if the Church Mattered*
Dietrich Bonhoeffer, *The Cost of Discipleship*
Robert Coleman, *The Master Plan of Evangelism*
James K. A. Smith, *You Are What You Love* & *Desiring the Kingdom*

The Rhythm of Fellowship

Brad House, *Community*
Steve Timmis and Tim Chester, *Total Church* & *Everyday Church*
Dietrich Bonheoffer, *Life Together*
Henry Cloud and John Townsend, *Making Small Groups Work*

The Rhythm of Scripture & Prayer

Eugene H. Peterson, *Answering God* & *Eat This Book*

Paul E. Miller, *A Praying Life*
Tim Keller, *Prayer*
Dallas Willard, *Hearing God*

The Rhythm of Hospitality

Tim Chester, *A Meal with Jesus*
Randy Frazee, *Making Room for Life*
Henri Nouwen, *Reaching Out*
Timothy J. Keller, "The Cost of Mission," Gospel in Life, Sermon preached October 30, 1994, www.gospelinlife.com/the-cost-of-mission.html

ACKNOWLEDGMENTS

Although I wrote this book by myself, it is the result of an entire community. I have had the privilege of working with community group leaders at three different churches: Karis Community Church in Columbia, MO (2007–2010), Sojourn Community Church in Louisville, KY (2010–2017), and Trinity Community Church in Columbia, MO (established 2017).

In particular, I'm thankful to Kevin Jamison, Brad House, and Daniel Montgomery for the opportunity to lead groups at Sojourn and for hundreds of hours of conversations about community. Several pastors and leaders of Sojourn East co-labored closely with me as we developed a groups ministry *in community*: Trey Kullman, Kyle and Hilary Noltemeyer, Ben Mast, Bert Guinn, Mark Franco, Jason Read, Mike Graham, Gregg and Nora Allison, James Santos, Chad Lewis, and Eric Johnson. My community pastor counterparts at the Midtown, J-Town, and New Albany congregations were equally helpful in sharpening my thinking on groups: Clif Roth, Josh Wilson, and Bobby Gilles.

My own community groups in Louisville from 2013–17 were the laboratories for most of the ideas and failures described in these pages. I want to especially thank Mark and Allison Wopata, Garrett and Nicole Pearson, Lindsey Poenie, and Dan and Abbie Rudibaugh for their eagerness to join Jessie and me in creating a life-giving community.

I also want to thank Dave Harvey, Justin Karl, Nick Weyrens, Michael Lee, and Casey Smith. Each made suggestions and improvements to this book. Their editorial work made this project infinitely more focused, concise and readable. Without them, it would be twice as long and half as helpful. Ain't nobody got time for that.

Most of all, I want to thank my darling wife, Jessie. She has been a model of hospitality, compassion, and perseverance as we have opened our home to dozens of people almost every week for the past eleven years. Our three boys (Joseph, Jude, and Jack) have grown up with a large group of friends, a regular rhythm of hospitality, and the best mama ever — I'm so thankful that they have experienced this type of childhood.

ABOUT THE AUTHOR

Jeremy Linneman is the lead pastor of Trinity Community Church in Columbia, Missouri. Prior to planting Trinity, he spent seven years as a community pastor of Sojourn Community Church in Louisville, Kentucky. He is the author of many articles and several short books and coaches leaders around the country.

He and his wife, Jessie, have been married for 12 years and have three sons. Connect with him at jslinneman.com.

ABOUT SOJOURN NETWORK

Throughout the pages of the New Testament, and especially in the book of Acts, we observe a pattern: men and women, through prayer and dependence of God and empowered by the Spirit, are sent by God (often through suffering) to spread the Word of the Lord. As this great news of new life in Christ spread into the neighboring cities, regions, provinces, and countries, gatherings of new believers formed into local communities called churches. As these gatherings formed by the thousands in the first century, the early church – taking its cue from the Scriptures — raised up qualified, called, and competent men to lead and shepherd these new congregations.

Two-thousand years later, God is still multiplying his gospel in and through his church, and the Good Shepherd is still using pastors to lead and shepherd God's people. In Sojourn Network, we desire to play our part in helping these pastors plant, grow, and multiply healthy churches.

We realize that only the Spirit can stir people's hearts and bring them into community with other believers in Jesus. Yet, by offering the pastors in our network a strong vision of planting, growing, and multiplying healthy churches and by providing them with thorough leadership assessment, funding for new churches and staff, coaching, training, renewal, and resources, we can best steward their gifts for the benefit and renewal of their local congregations.

Since 2011, our aim at Sojourn Network has been to provide the care and support necessary for our pastors to lead their churches with strength and joy — and to finish ministry well.

OTHER "HOW-TO" BOOKS

Here are the current books in the "How-To" series. Stay tuned for more.

Healthy Plurality = Durable Church: "How-To" Build and Maintain a Healthy Plurality of Elders by Dave Harvey

Life-Giving-Groups: "How-To" Grow Healthy, Multiplying Community Groups by Jeremy Linneman

Charting the Course: "How-To" Navigate the Legal Side of a Church Plant by Tim Beltz

Redemptive Participation: A "How-To" Guide for Pastors in Culture by Mike Cosper

Filling Blank Spaces: "How-To" Work with Visual Artists in Your Church by Michael Winters

Before the Lord, Before the Church: "How-To" Plan a Child Dedication Service by Jared Kennedy with Megan Kennedy

Sabbaticals: "How-To" Take a Break from Ministry before Ministry Breaks You by Rusty McKie

Leaders through Relationship: "How-To" Develop Leaders in the Local Church by Kevin Galloway

Raising the Dust: "How-To" Equip Deacons to Serve the Church by Gregg Allison & Ryan Welsh (forthcoming)

Healthy Plurality = Durable Church: "How-To" Build and Maintain a Healthy Plurality of Elders by Dave Harvey

Have you ever wondered what separates a healthy church from an unhealthy church when they have the same doctrine (and even methods) on paper? The long-term health and durability of a church simply cannot exceed the health of her elders who lead, teach, shepherd, and pray the church forward. Therefore, building and maintaining a healthy plurality of elders is the key to durability. Yet a healthy plurality is a delicate thing working through hardship and the difficulties of relationship while pursuing the noble task of eldership. If you wish to grow deeper in your theology of eldership to lead with a healthy, biblical vision of plurality, then this is your "How-To" guide.

Life-Giving-Groups: "How-To" Grow Healthy, Multiplying Community Groups by Jeremy Linneman

Cultivate life-giving, Christ-centered communities. After many years of leading small groups and coaching hundreds of small group leaders, pastor and writer Jeremy Linneman has come to a bold conviction: Community groups are the best place for us — as relational beings — to become mature followers of Christ. This short book seeks to answer two questions: How can our community groups cultivate mature disciples of Christ? And how can our groups grow and multiply to sustain a healthy church? Whether you are new to community groups or tired from years of challenging ministry, *Life-Giving Groups* is a fresh, practical invitation to life together in Christ.

Charting the Course: "How-To" Navigate the Legal Side of a Church Plant by Tim Beltz

Planting a church? It's time to plot the course toward legal validity.
Church planting is overwhelming enough before dealing with the legal and business regulations of founding a church. *Charting the Course* is for anyone, at any experience level to learn how to navigate the legal side of planting a church.

Redemptive Participation: A "How-To" Guide for Pastors in Culture by Mike Cosper

Our culture is confused. And so are we. It's not just you or them. It's all of us. But we can move past confusion and into a place of careful discernment. *Redemptive Participation* brings awareness to the shaping forces in our current culture and how to connect these dynamics with our teaching and practice.

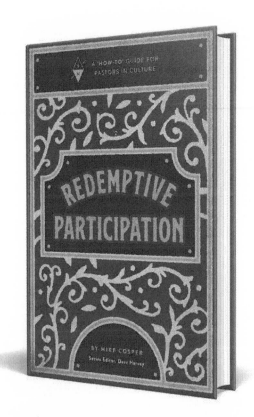

Filling Blank Spaces: "How-To" Work with Visual Artists in Your Church by Michael Winters

In the beginning, the earth was empty. Blank spaces were everywhere. *Filling Blank Spaces* addresses a topic that usually gets blank stares in the church world. But Winters is a seasoned veteran of arts ministry and has developed a premier arts and culture movement in the United States, without elaborate budgets or celebrity cameos. Instead, this guide gives a "How-To" approach to understanding visual art as for and from the local church, steering clear of both low-brow kitsch and obscure couture. If you are ready to start engaging a wider, and often under-reached, swath of your city, while awakening creative force within your local church, then this book is for you.

Before the Lord, Before the Church: "How-To" Plan a Child Dedication Service by Jared Kennedy with Megan Kennedy

Is child dedication just a sentimental moment to celebrate family with "oohs and ahhs" over the babies? Or is it a solemn moment before God and a covenanting one before the local church? Kennedy explains a philosophy of child dedication with poignant "How-To" plan for living out a powerful witness to Christ for one another and before the watching world. Whether you are rescuing various forms of child dedication from sentimentalism or perhaps sacrament, this book will guide you to faithful and fruitful ministry honoring God for the gift of children while blessing your church.

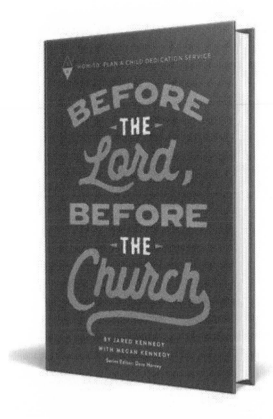

Sabbaticals: "How-To" Take a Break from Ministry before Ministry Breaks You by Rusty McKie

Are you tired and worn out from ministry? Isn't Jesus' burden supposed to be light? In the pressure-producing machine of our chaotic world, Jesus' words of rest don't often touch our life. As ministry leaders, we know a lot about biblical rest, yet we don't often experience it. The ancient practice of sabbath provides ample wisdom on how to enter into rest in Christ. *Sabbaticals* is a guide showing us how to implement Sabbath principles into a sabbatical as well as into the ebb and flow of our entire life.

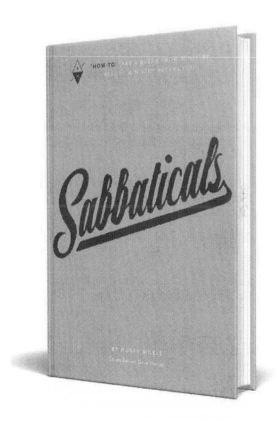

Leaders through Relationship: "How-To" Develop Leaders in the
Local Church by Kevin Galloway

The church needs more godly leaders. But where do they come from?
Some people read leadership books in a season of rest and health. But if
we're honest, most often we read leadership books when we're frazzled,
when we see the problems around us but not the solutions. If you're feeling
the leadership strain in your church, let Kevin Galloway show you a way
forward, the way of Jesus, the way of personally investing in leaders who
then invest in other leaders—because making an intentional plan to
encourage and train leaders, is not a luxury; it's mission critical, for your
health and the health of your church.

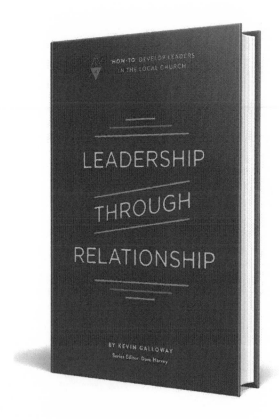

Raising the Dust: "How-To" Equip Deacons to Serve the Church by Gregg Allison & Ryan Welsh (forthcoming)

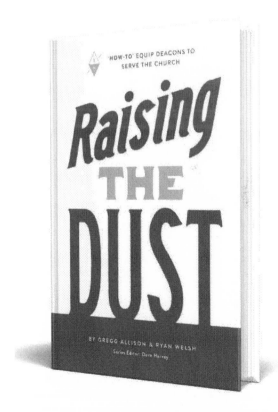